Raising Mom

Mereo Books

2nd Floor, 6-8 Dyer Street, Cirencester, Gloucestershire, GL7 2PF
An imprint of Memoirs Books. www.mereobooks.com
and www.memoirsbooks.co.uk

Raising Mom
ISBN: 978-1-86151-857-6

First published in Great Britain in 2024
by Mereo Books, an imprint of Memoirs Books.

Copyright ©2024

Jane Farrell has asserted his right under the Copyright Designs and
Patents Act 1988 to be identified as the author of this work.

A CIP catalogue record for this book is available from the British Library.
This book is sold subject to the condition that it shall not by way of trade or otherwise be lent,
resold, hired out or otherwise circulated without the publisher's prior consent in any form of
binding or cover, other than that in which it is published and without a similar condition, including
this condition being imposed on the subsequent purchaser.

The address for Memoirs Books can be
found at www.mereobooks.com

Mereo Books Ltd. Reg. No. 12157152

Typeset in 13/20pt Garamond
by Wiltshire Associates.
Printed and bound in Great Britain

Raising Mom

A Daughter's Gift for her Mother's Final Days

Jane Farrell

CONTENTS

Introduction

Raising Us 1

Becoming Dependent 5

Flowers and Clams 9

Watching Planes 13

Chair Exercises 14

September 2023 16

Going with the Flo 17

Tell Me Your Life Story 19

October 2023 22

Heart Trouble 26

A Hospital Visit 29

Sleepless Nights 31

Respite 34

Christmas Time 37

The Last Chapter: In Hospice Care 41

Epilogue 47

INTRODUCTION

◆———◆

Full circle. Your parents raise you, care for you, teach you, all in hopes of building your strength, character, and faith. Then, as we turn into adults with our own families, we take that advice, follow or reject it accordingly, and adjust to create our own lives. And we tend to support the political party our parents did, celebrate holidays the same way they did, and even store our kitchen items in the same cabinets as they did. With this knowledge, we need to move forward with some of their advice and find our own way.

And this is true with our own children; as much as we try to guide them, intentionally or in the moment, there is only a certain amount that sticks. They need to find their own way, as we all do.

And so as we grow older, our roles and responsibilities change. We're sandwiched someplace in between raising our own children and escorting our parents into their old age. The house I live in now is the home I grew up in, and my childhood bedroom, which was later my daughter's bedroom when she was younger, now belongs to my mother. In a way, I am now raising Mom here.

My parents, Florence and Steve, married in 1959 and were part of a more old-fashioned generation. My mother stayed home to 'keep house' and raise the children, while my father was the 'breadwinner'. However, they each took on these roles while respecting the other's contributions and always working as a team. In speaking with others about their childhoods, undoubtedly, I'm lucky to have had the parents that I did. They were generous, supportive, and loving. I have no doubt they loved each other, and the fortuitous events that brought them together, not-so-spontaneously meeting at a Hungarian dance, proved to create a beautiful, love-filled marriage. Theirs was a marriage full of love and respect.

Don't get me wrong; there were moments when I heard them argue. These disagreements, I feel, were fueled by the stressors and expectations of that era, along with two people trying to meld into one, while keeping their distinct personalities and preferences. This seems to be true for all the decades to follow. We all come with baggage that impacts the person we become and our decisions and responses. Two people trying to stuff both of their full bags into one suitcase is nearly impossible.

Raising Us

❖──❖

My parents gave my sister Lynn and me a wonderful life full of love, support, and generosity, none of which we took for granted, but always returned tenfold. When they took us out to dinner, we always made sure to say thank you. They paid our way through college and bought each of us a new car on our eighteenth birthday. Unlike the birthday parties of today, in a rented venue, with entertainment, we had a simpler version. A party at our house, with a craft (Mom loved découpage and needlepoint), some pin-the-tail-on-the-donkey, a homemade cake, and a goody bag.

Dad worked hard to provide for his family. He served in the Navy during peacetime, but never went to college. Initially, he worked at the drycleaning business that his parents owned. Then when drycleaning went out of favor, he went to work in the textile business as a salesman. My mom was a stay-at-home mom. Before they wed, she was a secretary/bookkeeper and did very well for herself, ahead of her time as a working woman. She was always dressed to the nines, very classy, and even bought herself a diamond cocktail ring which she has recently passed on to me.

My mother, Florence, was raised in a large family; not many siblings, but lots of aunts and uncles. She would always tell stories of the Christmases they shared and how the family all lived close by. She would recount how the children would go house to house with their parents on Christmas Eve, collecting the gifts given by each family.

Growing up, my Christmases were filled with family, delicious food, music, and lots of gifts. Our family tradition was to exchange gifts with aunts and uncles on Christmas Eve. It was not a sit-down dinner, but an array of appetizers. Christmas morning my sister Lynn and I would open the presents from our parents (aka Santa). I would wake Lynn at the crack of dawn because I was so excited to see what "Santa" had brought me and if I had got everything I asked for. Family would arrive in the afternoon and we would all enjoy a turkey dinner with all the trimmings together. Everything was homemade.

My father, Steve, died at any early age, sixty-two, from cancer. This was a very difficult time. My sister had already married and left the family home. I still lived at home with my parents and was newly engaged. I was happy that my dad got to meet my fiancé, but their time getting to know one another was limited. Sadly, my father passed before our wedding. I was thankful that he at least got to meet my future husband, Ken. When I showed my father my ring, he kissed it and gave me a big hug. Some people said I should move the wedding forward, but to me that would be like saying to my dad "you're not going to make it".

I was proud of my mom for being able to handle the bills and maintain her home without my dad. My mother stayed in the family home for a few years after my father's passing and then moved down to the Jersey shore to be near her sister. She offered to sell our family home to Ken and me, a home that they designed and had built for them, and we heartily agreed. It was in a town we could not afford to buy a home in, and it was a loving home filled with beautiful memories. I was not sure whether it would truly ever feel like our home, but with all our furniture and personal items moved in, it became ours, with the added benefit of being filled with beautiful memories and love.

Becoming Dependent

⊶ · ⊷

As the years passed, Mom enjoyed living in her home, close to her sister Helen, my aunt, knowing that the family home was passed on to my husband Ken and me. Even after my aunt passed, my mother continued to live in her own house, and we enjoyed visiting often. But as she got older, it was clear she could no longer live on her own. I had to take her car away as she had glaucoma, and it was getting worse. She was not happy, even though she only used the car to go food shopping. But still it meant her independence was decreasing. While in the past she took care of all her bills, now she would put bills aside in the laundry room and forget about them but would always make sure to donate to Wounded Warriors. I would need to clean out her refrigerator and pantry often, as many of the items had expired. Her health insurance lapsed twice for lack of payment.

At this time, I found a senior living development very close to my home and moved her there. At first, she was not happy with this arrangement and missed her house. I had to make decisions to keep her safe and cared for, as I'm sure she did for me as I was growing up. Change is never easy, especially when you're her age. However, eventually she would say how much she loved her "little apartment". My sister Lynn and I brought whatever we could from her former home to make it as personal and homey as possible. It was a small one-bedroom apartment, so we couldn't bring a lot, but we managed to make it a place she was comfortable in with many of her treasured things around her.

I arranged for her doctors to visit her there, as getting her out to a doctor's office was a bit of a process. The doctor would check her physically, but they also did cognitive testing. They asked her what day it was, what year it was, what time of year, and other questions. Most of the time she did not know the answer. But at her age, with no schedule to abide by, there really was no reason for her to know what day it was.

There was a button that she had to press every morning by 10:30 to let the facility know she was okay. She continually forgot to do this, despite the multiple notes I put around to remind her, so the front desk would often call her to see if she was ok.

After five years, when she was ninety-six, it was apparent that she could not stay there by herself anymore. She did not leave her apartment to socialize or dine and spent most of her days sitting on her couch watching TV and eating ice cream. I would bring her leftovers and they would still be in the refrigerator a week later. I was afraid to bring her anything that she needed to use the stove for, as there was an incident when she left something in a pot on the stove with the burner on and set off the fire alarm. So I would bring her things like yogurt, cottage cheese, milk, Ensures (a chocolate shake with vitamins) and orange juice. And of course, lots of ice cream. The option of putting her in assisted living or having live-in help was quickly dismissed, as this was not something she would have wanted.

Which brings me to the present. Mom is moving in with me part-time, and with my sister part-time. We know that it will be a big undertaking, so we want to share the time, also knowing that this will be time we will each be able to spend with Mom. Lynn lives only about a half-hour away, so it seems like a viable arrangement. As much as we tried to explain this arrangement to Mom, she would often forget.

Flowers and Clams

·▶-·-◀·

Mom's memory is fading, but she reminisces often and will repeat the same stories over and over: "I remember Daddy would come home from work. I would be cooking at the stove, and he'd come in the side door with flowers. Sometimes he would stop at the fish market and get some clams, which he knew I loved. So romantic," she jokes. They traveled a lot - Aruba, Italy, Austria, Hungary, and various destinations in the United States. Almost every Friday night they would go out to dinner. I'm so glad they got to do all these things before my dad passed and didn't wait until he retired. Tomorrow is promised to no one.

She often talks about the day she met my father. She went to a Hungarian dance with her family. The story goes that the two families had a friend in common and the meeting may not have been so unplanned. She smiles as she recalls walking into the room and seeing "a bunch of fellas" standing by the wall. Her eyes went straight to my dad, and she saw that he too had noticed her. He asked her to dance, picking her up and twirling her at the end. "Everybody laughed," she adds with a reminiscent smile.

She talks a lot about my dad's family in Hungary and her visits there. "We took them out to dinner in Budapest to a fancy restaurant," she recalls. "First, we sat at the bar and had a drink. And there was a small band playing Hungarian music. I was so moved that I started to cry. They became concerned that I was upset, but I explained that they were tears of joy."

Our Hungarian cousins were from a small town, Tès, with fresh eggs from their chickens, and cows that walked down the dirt road to the fields daily. My mom always recounts how the cows would all walk down the dirt road to the pasture every day, and when they returned, they all knew which house to go to. It was a simple but happy life. So, as you can imagine, our Hungarian relatives were just as moved and impressed by the Budapest dinner as my mom was.

When our Hungarian cousins came to visit the United States, they were in awe that the supermarkets had entire aisles for pets. My parents took them into New York City to see a musical on Broadway. I don't recall which one, but it was something where the fact that they did not speak the language did not matter. My mom recalls walking out of the theatre down the steps, an opulent chandelier above them, and once again being brought to tears. "I was impressed," she remembers. "I can only imagine how they felt."

Almost two weeks into her stay with me, Mom is always asking, "What can I do for you?" She wants to be helpful and to have something to do. At her apartment, she basically did nothing but sit on the couch and watch TV all day. So why she wants to keep busy here feels unusual to me. I think she just wants to be useful and "earn her keep". So she and I do wash a lot and I let her do the folding of the towels and the clothes. For Mom, this is an art. She will take three to four minutes to fold a nightgown that will end up being smushed into a drawer. But she enjoys it and it gives her purpose. She also enjoys playing on her iPad, Candy Crush and the like. Solitaire is one she is particularly good at. Sometimes we will play cards or Rummikub.

Watching Planes

◆━━◆

Heading into week three, when the weather is good, we sit out on the deck in the backyard. Luckily, there is currently a flight pattern that takes the planes heading for Teterboro and Newark Airport directly over my house. This is something my mother loves, watching the planes overhead. She's scared to fly but loves to watch them fly by. She remarks at how many there are and that they are all going the same way, "like it's a road in the sky". We'll enjoy a cocktail and some cheese and crackers together. Inevitably, she falls asleep eventually. When the weather turns cold, we don't go out to the deck, but she still longs to be out there.

Chair Exercises

❖—❖

After being sedentary for the last twenty years of her life, especially the last five, Mom is stiff and struggles to get around. For five years, she sat on the couch in her apartment, did not leave for dinner, and did not socialize, take part in activities, or even sit outside. So, getting up, getting down, movement in any way is a struggle. So, this week, we embark on chair exercises for seniors. We begin with a ten-minute easy workout on YouTube. I initially do it with her.

"You don't have to do this, you're not old," she says.

I reassure her that any movement would benefit me, especially after having shoulder surgery. Soon, I will have her do the exercise on her own. The only problem with this is that sometimes she will sit with her arms folded, merely watching, as if this is a new movie, or she will pick up her iPad and begin to play. So out of the ten minutes, there might be seven minutes of exercise, but she's working hard.

After ten minutes, she will say, "Wow, that's really a workout."

But alas, her sense of humor comes through at the most unexpected moments, like once when she was struggling to get up out of the chair on the deck to go inside, and I jokingly said, "Well, maybe next time you're doing exercises, you'll pay more attention."

Her response was "Blah, blah, blah, blah, blah!"

September 2023

❖——❖

Now it is time for Ken and me to return to work. We both work in the education field. That means that Mom will be alone from 8:30 a.m. to 3:00 p.m. every Monday through Friday. I'm a little nervous about this, but she already had been alone at the senior living apartment, so I figure it will be OK.

The first day I am not sure what I will find when I come home from work, but Mom is sitting at the kitchen table, dressed, watching TV, and playing on her iPad. We had left breakfast out for her and told her about lunch. She did not remember to eat lunch, which is fine. She has become used to eating very little and as she gets older she does not eat as much as she used to. Most afternoons we will have a small snack, cheese and crackers or pretzels. I am relieved that she was able to spend the day on her own.

Going with the Flo

⇢──⇠

As carefully as we've planned a schedule for Mom to stay at my house and my sister's, there are times when we need to tweak it for certain events. Lynn and I are flexible. Mom is not. Upon my returning to work, Mom is staying with Lynn. She has come back to my house just for a weekend, as Lynn has plans and does not want to leave Mom alone. Mom doesn't understand the change and forgot that we told her multiple times about it. Explaining to her that she'll be going back to my sister's in a few days will be equally confusing to her. I imagine she likes being "settled" somewhere.

I have to believe in my heart that this new living arrangement must be better than her sitting on a couch alone in her apartment eating ice cream for dinner and watching Fox News. I am sure she appreciates it, and she seems to be happy. However, it can be hard on her transitioning back and forth and going with the "Flo."

Tell Me Your Life Story

◆→ ←◆

My mom received a book as a present entitled "Tell Me your Life Story". In it are various questions about growing up, family, friends, achievements, etc. By this time, her memories are already fading, so we are eager to document her answers. Some she knows right away, others she cannot remember, and others she remembers with some coaching.

When asked about any struggles her family may have had growing up, she recounts (with prompting) how her father was an air raid sergeant. She says there was a period of time when there were a lot of sirens, and "it was serious for a while". She and Helen would laugh about her dad having to walk up and down the street at night.

She also recalls how she and Helen were born only

about fourteen months apart, but could not have been more different. Mom has always been very studious, prim, and proper, and her sister was a bit of a rebel, very funny. Mom took piano lessons, and Helen would make faces at her to make her laugh. Helen was affectionately called 'Sis' by everyone.

Mom delights in saying that when she went to church, the congregation could not wait for her to enter so that they could see her outfit. She was always dressed to the nines. "I had a good job and bought nice clothes," she says.

When asked to describe herself, she replies, "Screwball," and laughs aloud. She adds that she thinks she was a good parent. She and my dad were very close friends with a couple they knew. They would travel together and play cards on the weekends. She says, "I never thought I would be the last one alive". Her feelings are equal parts surprise and sadness that they are no longer here.

Looking back, she says she wishes she had more time with family and that the two most important things to her are close friends and close family.

"I've lived a good life," she says. "I've been to a lot of

places and experienced a lot of things."

And I always reply that she has been so lucky and that most people cannot say that. I only wish she'd had more time with my dad. One of her best memories is the day they married.

When asked "What was the most stressful time in your life?" she responds, "You always have days when you are stressed about things. I never had something dramatic in my life. Nothing that I could not get over in a short time."

October 2023

◆—◆

Mom is on the decline. Her breathing is labored, with a cough and some wheezing. She sleeps a lot, and her ankles are swollen. After taking her to our primary care doctor, it was determined that she was in atrial fibrillation, heart failure, with a high risk of stroke. I have taken a leave of absence from my job to care for her. There is no way I would feel comfortable leaving her alone all day. Now her breathing is better, no wheezing, and she has lost about five pounds of fluid. However, her blood pressure is on the low side, perhaps due to too many diuretics.

The next day she visits a cardiologist who puts her on three new meds: blood thinners, a diuretic for the swelling, and an additional medication for the elevated blood pressure. She also must wear a heart monitor for two weeks. The first night, she takes it off, we reapply it, and then it falls off. This happens a few more times. We take her blood pressure and pulse daily and weigh her to make sure the diuretics are working and she is not gaining more fluid weight.

Mom is increasingly out of breath after doing the slightest tasks. Getting dressed and taking a shower are an extreme effort. Today I took her to get her haircut. When we got home, she watched a movie and drank an Ensure. As expected, she was asleep after not too long. When I have to wake her up from a daytime nap, it is nearly impossible. She is just so tired. I woke her up at 5:00 because I wanted her to eat something and take her pills. She just wanted to go to her bed. I eventually got her to the kitchen, where she could barely keep her head up, while I fed her some soup and a few small bites of a buttered roll.

At 6:15 she was in bed. I turned on YouTube, to a channel that played Andrea Bocelli, her favorite, but she was asleep within minutes. Tomorrow, we will take her to the hospital. One good thing: she still has her sense of humor. When I asked if she needed her cane to get to the bathroom, she said, "I could fly," and then began to laugh.

Sunday, we decide to take Mom to the hospital. Her breathlessness, wheezing, swollen legs, and excessive sleeping are concerning. We went back and forth on whether to do this, but I am glad we decided to take her. The doctors and nurses at the hospital are so friendly, caring, and attentive. This definitely tends to relieve some of the doubt and fear. The best, though, is that my daughter Katelyn, Mom's granddaughter, is a social worker at the hospital in the cardiac wing. I do not know what I would do without her calmness, or rapport with the staff, and her knowledge of the process. Not to mention her attention to Mom.

The doctors decide that Mom should stay the night at the hospital to get rid of some of the fluid, and an echocardiogram would be done in the morning. Mom is annoyed by the pulse oximeter and complains about the IV. She continually tries to remove it, so the nurse has put gauze around it to prevent this. She has a private room with all my daughter's co-workers taking extra good care of her.

On Day 3 in the hospital, it looks like she will be staying another day or so. A lot of fluid has been removed from her body and her heart rate has been lowered with medication. She always says she is not a bit hungry, but when the food is put in front of her, she eats it all. Her favorite at the hospital? The salmon. "I'm going to bring the rest home and have it tomorrow," she says. Of course, she never says no to ice cream. She wants to come home and I want her home too, but not until she is ready.

I visit Mom daily, although most of the time she is sleeping. The sound of patients in other rooms continuously calling for the nurse, moaning, and televisions blaring soon become background noise. The monotonous sound of the heart monitor and the intermittent clicking of the IV stay with me long after I've left the hospital, along with the recurring *Code Blue* over the loudspeaker, only tempered by the occasional few notes of *Lullaby* each time a baby is born.

Heart Trouble

◆→ ─ ◆◆

By Day 4, the hospital has become more familiar than I would want such a place to feel. I thought Mom would have been discharged by now, but her numbers are still not where they should be. Different doctors and specialists are recommending various procedures, one of which is a cardioversion, a technique to get her heart back into rhythm. This involves inserting a small camera down her throat so they can see the back of her heart, a place where the echocardiogram cannot see. This is to ensure that there are no clots. Then they would be able to do the cardioversion, which involves shocking her heart back into rhythm. This initial camera operation has its own risks. And she must be on blood thinners for three more weeks before they can do it. It is possible her heart will go back into normal rhythm all on its own, or they can use medication to assist.

Ultimately, on the advice and assurance from another cardiologist who would perform the cardioversion that the procedure would help, not be risky, and was very routine, we decide this is the best course of action. Mom is brought down to the cardiac catheterization lab, where I wait with her. I play one of her favorite songs on my phone, "Bésame Mucho" by Andrea Bocelli. When I have to leave her, I go to the chapel for a brief moment, and then wait for the call. I don't even know what to ask God for. Only twenty minutes later, the procedure is done. It is a success.

So now Mom is home again with me. We have a visiting nurse, physical therapist, and dietician coming to the house to check in on her. The nurse comes twice a week, checks her vitals and her medications. The physical therapist has given her some exercises to do and showed her safe and easier ways to get up and down from a chair. We must watch her carefully, her blood pressure, her pulse, the swelling in her legs. This is all recorded on an iPad that connects to a monitoring center. In addition, I keep copious notes on her blood pressure, weight, and medication. Medical terms creep into my vocabulary. Turns out the cardioversion offered only temporary correction; Mom is back in AFib again.

I try to give Mom small tasks, but since she has been home from the hospital, I am very careful not to have her overexert herself. She likes to fold towels and clothes, but now I give her only small garments and washcloths that she can fold while sitting down. She also likes to dry the dishes in the dish drain, so we try to make sure there are none in there or that we remove all the heavy pots and let her dry only the small items. She repeats how she does not want to be a burden or a nuisance, and she gets frustrated with herself and her situation. So, it is important that I let her do as much as she can by herself and let her feel her purpose and value to being here. It is a finely tuned, ever changing dance, almost a balancing act, making sure she is safe physically and happy mentally.

A Hospital Visit

❖⋯❖

Last night Mom felt nauseous and had a stomach ache. I made salmon for dinner, but just gave her some soup so as not to upset her stomach more. Upon getting into bed for the evening, she vomited and was shaking. She then seemed fine, so she went to bed.

Early in the morning she gets up to go to the bathroom and can hardly walk. It takes me and my husband together to get her there. It seems like she cannot lift her feet. Ken and I confer, and decide she needs to go to the hospital. This time, though, we cannot drive her there. There is no way we can get her out of the house and down the stairs, even though there are only four steps.

I text my sister at 6:00 a.m. explaining the situation and asking her to come to the house. She replies that she will get dressed and come right over. In the meantime, my husband calls for an ambulance. A police officer is the first to arrive. Turns out I recognize him and realize I work with his brother. He is very warm, friendly, and funny, putting us all at ease and joking with Mom. Then it seems like the cavalry has arrived. Paramedics, EMT, ambulance; there are eight people in my house. My sister and I get in her car and head to the hospital, while Ken stays with Mom by the ambulance until they evaluate her and head to the hospital.

She has a slight fever, so there is a suspicion that she has an infection. Urinalysis, chest X-ray and Covid test prove negative. She also is sent for a CAT scan because she had fallen the week before and has a large hematoma on her rear. She is admitted, once again on the floor on which my daughter is a social worker. She stays overnight and is released the next day as her cardiac symptoms are under control.

Mom is happy to be home and is feeling and sounding much better. Her vitals are within range, she is eating and sleeping well, and the swelling in her legs has subsided.

Sleepless Nights

❖ ❖

I do not sleep. I have never been a good sleeper, but now I feel like I am sleeping as I did when my children were babies, always wondering if I heard them stirring or crying, getting up to check anyway to make sure they were okay. This was especially true with my younger daughter, Katelyn. She was born with a heart defect that required open-heart surgery at the age of three months. Up until she was about four years old, I would go into her room every night after she fell asleep and listen for her breath and look for the rise and fall of her chest to make sure she was breathing.

Now I wonder if I hear my mom coughing, or getting out of bed, walking down the hallway to the bathroom. My main concern is her getting in and out of bed by herself or falling on the way to the bathroom. We have a railing on the side of the bed to keep her from falling out, but it sometimes makes it difficult to get in and out of bed. We've also lowered the mattress to make it easier for her to navigate.

With that in mind, I purchased a mini camera that connects to an app on my phone. It has worked well, alerting me to any movement in Mom's room, and a view to what she is doing. This way I do not have to wonder if I heard something. However, I still sometimes have to get up and assist her because she will take her cane, instead of the much more stable walker.

The past four weeks has seemed like six months. There is no time to be off duty. It's a 24-hour job. I know Mom appreciates it, as she tells me often, "You take such good care of me. I don't know why." And I tell her, "Because you're my mommy and I love you". She forgets things often, sometimes within seconds, and the repetition can be exhausting. When I feel the frustration rise, I remind myself that it is not her fault.

I will be going back to work on November 28th. For several reasons. One, this time with my mom has been so rewarding and special, but also draining. I feel like I need a break to regroup to take care of Mom for the next round. I also feel like I abandoned my colleagues and students. Sure, probably most of them do not even care that I' m not there, but I hope I made some type of positive impression in the month that I was with them at the start of the school year. I do not know how Mom will react to the new schedule of being at my sister's, but we are trying to do what is best for everyone.

Mom is sleeping more. She will go to bed at around 8:00 p.m. and then wake up two or three times during the night to use the bathroom. But once she is up for the day, there's a more than likely chance that she'll fall asleep at the kitchen table or on the chair in her bedroom, for two, three, four hours. I have tried to wake her up for fear that she would then not sleep at night, but trying to wake her up before she is ready is futile. And I have found that despite all that daytime napping she will still sleep at night. The AFib is making her tired. And let us not forget, she is ninety-seven years old.

Respite

◆──◆

Mom is at my sister's for a few days, as Ken and I had plans in the city. We go to Birdland Jazz Club and see Jane Monheit, a jazz singer. It's a fabulous evening, well needed. Then on Saturday we go out to dinner and drinks in the city. It is a nice respite and we both feel rejuvenated. Ken has been such an integral part of Mom's care and such a great source of strength for me. He has a wonderful relationship with her and they like to joke around. He makes sure to get her a jelly donut every Sunday and she finishes every bite.

But Mom is increasingly out of breath. A short walk to the bathroom and back leaves her breathless. When she gets into bed at night it is a process. And when she lays her head down on the pillows (I have several to keep her head raised) she seems out of breath.

"I can barely breathe," she says, and I do the breathing exercises with her; in through the nose like you are smelling a flower, out through the mouth like you are blowing out a candle. She seems frightened as we do this. After, her eyes seem teary, and she seems down. I cannot imagine what she is thinking.

I have decorated her bedroom for Christmas. There is a small tabletop tree that she had in her apartment that I've put in her room with all her ornaments. Over the years, she's collected Annalee figurine dolls, a collection of mice dressed for different holidays. She must have about twenty, for Easter, Halloween, Thanksgiving, Fourth of July, and of course Christmas.

The end of November, the date I chose to go back to work, is approaching quickly. After Mom was in the hospital, I did not want to move her back and forth from my house to my sister's until she was stable. After having a visiting nurse and physical therapist come to our home to monitor her and take her vitals daily during the month of October and early November, I feel comfortable that she can move on to stay with Lynn after two months with me. I need to go back to work, not only for myself, but so I can be re-energized to care for Mom in a meaningful way.

I have made the right decision about going back to work. I need to feel a part of a team again and be with colleagues and friends. With that, I miss my mom and feel bad that she is not with me at my house. I text Lynn every other day to see if I can facetime with Mom, and every time Mom is sleeping. Lately, my sister reports that Mom is getting worse, sleeping more, unstable on her feet, out of breath. And now Mom seems scared. The other night she asked Lynn to check on her after she went to bed.

Christmas Time

◆—◆

Mom is staying with me for the holiday week. There is a marked difference in her health. She is sleeping constantly and not eating. Getting in and out of bed and walking takes everything out of her. She finds it hard to catch her breath. She slept through Christmas Eve. Christmas morning, I am able to get her out of bed and dressed before the rest of my family joins us for the holiday. She sits with us in the living room but is asleep most of the time and does not eat dinner. We are able to get her to come sit at the table with us for dessert where she has a tiny sliver of peanut butter pie and a glass of milk. All she wants to do is get back in bed.

The day after Christmas we decide to once again take her to the hospital, as her condition is worsening. She is dressed and sitting in the kitchen when the police officers and the ambulance arrive. Getting her on the stretcher and to the ambulance is frightening and heartbreaking as she is crying out, not in pain, but in fear. I accompany her in the ambulance to the hospital to try to make her more comfortable. I am so impressed with the calmness and kindness of the police officers and EMTs.

It was not an easy decision to take Mom to the hospital. It is not the place we want her to be, or she wants to be, but she needs to be there. From our perspective we only surmise this by observing her. She does not ever complain. She is dehydrated and beginning kidney failure. She also has a pleural effusion in her lungs. Her blood pressure and pulse need to be regulated. So it was the right decision.

***

Today is Day 2 of Mom's stay in the hospital. She is receiving fluids to address the dehydration, but not so much as to negatively affect the heart. A fine line. Her vitals are improving. However, she is still sleeping constantly. This morning, she woke up for a little bit and had a few bites of breakfast. Today they did an abdominal X-ray as her stomach is distended and she is not passing enough urine. Tomorrow they will drain the fluid from her lungs.

***

The procedure to drain the fluid from her lungs was a success. They were able to remove over a liter of fluid. That should make it easier for her to breathe. In addition, that fluid caused her to have excess CO_2 in her blood, which contributed to her confusion and lethargy. However, her heart rate increased during the night, so they put her on a Cardizem drip for the second time. This morning, they took her off the drip and gave her a pill instead. She has been taking her pills crushed in chocolate ice cream. She never says no to ice cream.

Today she is awake for lunch and I am able to feed her some chicken broth, which she eats most of, and my sister feeds her chocolate ice cream. She does open her eyes from time to time, but more often she is sleeping and it is difficult to wake her up. After speaking to the social worker, conferring with my daughter, and the hospice representative, Mom is evaluated for hospice and the decision is made to go ahead with that option. Being in the hospital three times in three months is an indication that the issues will continue to return and there is not much else the hospital can do for her. The A-fib is exhausting her, and as Lynn put it, "her heart is tired". She continues to sleep most of the day and night.

Mom will go to my sister's, since Ken and I both work. I am so torn by this because I know it is a lot to take on for anyone, but I know Lynn will have help, both from family and outside sources. Mom's vitals are under control with meds, and she is off the oxygen. The big hurdle will be getting her to the bathroom and showering her. Most of the time she is sleeping. Still, I feel I want her here with me and I mourn that she'll probably never be in my house again.

I have brought pictures of my father that I had in Mom's room here for my sister to keep in Mom's room at her house. I am trying to do all I can to assure Lynn that she can do this and that she will have support. I have made chicken soup, cream of asparagus soup, and banana muffins for her to keep in her freezer for Mom. I plan to visit at least once a week.

The Last Chapter: In Hospice Care

❖⸺❖

Mom is transported to my sister's house by ambulette. I pick up her new meds and head there after I leave the hospital. My daughter also comes by to visit. The hospice nurse arrives and evaluates Mom. She says she looks so much better than she expected based on the medical reports. The hospice worker is kind, gentle and reassuring. When Lynn asks if she could give a prognosis or timeline, the nurse states that time in a hospice is usually six months.

"With your mom, I would say half that. And if I can be frank, I would say a month."

As devastating as that is to hear, we at least have a chance to prepare ourselves and we want to be assured that Mom would not suffer.

RAISING MOM

The hospice nurse in charge of Mom's case is here today and supplies are delivered. In addition, a chaplain visits. They are both so nice and gentle with Mom, and compassionate but honest with us. They assure us we are not alone and that we can call any time and that they will be visiting multiple times a week. The hospice nurse explains that at this point Mom will probably start seeing people who have already passed. She said Mom might wait for a certain significant date to let go, or that she might not want us to be in the room when she passes.

There are more and more physical signs that Mom's body is shutting down. After speaking to the hospice nurse, she indicates that these signs point to kidney failure, which probably gives us one week. It is happening so fast, but we don't want her to linger.

When she is awake and talking, which is rare, it's a bit of gibberish, like she can't find the words and get them out. When it is intelligible, it is things like "exercise," I need to go shopping," and talking about her Coach bags.

She is saying no to ice cream.

Mom is opening her eyes less and less. But we continue to talk to her and play music for her. Based on her condition, the hospice nurse feels it will be only a few days. I have once again stopped working and basically moved into my sister's house to be with her and near Mom. At one point, Mom seemed to be waving at someone and then reached out her hand as if to grab hold of someone. She muttered the word "sister" so clearly that even the hospice nurse understood her. It's so important to me that she feels safe now and knows we're here, so I make sure to talk to her and touch her often.

* * *

It's Friday, and it is clear that the end is nearing. The nurse suggests we call a priest for last rites for Mom. Multiple people make calls to two different churches in the area that my sister is affiliated with, and get no response. The nurse conveys that it seems that Mom is holding on for some reason. We do not know what, but we want to cover all our bases. As a eucharistic minister, I suggest that I could anoint Mom. Of course, the last rights are something I am not qualified to do, but we knew what we had to do. I prepare a prayer and a reading. Lynn has holy water from Lourdes. Anything we can do to make Mom feel safe, secure, and loved is what we will do.

Initially, I want to wait until the home health aide leaves at five o'clock for more privacy, but earlier in the day I felt like I was going to jump out of my skin and was feeling so uncomfortable. My mom opened her eyes a few times, but clearly could not see. I did not want to wait. So around 2:00 we gather around Mom, say the prayers, including the Our Father, and anoint Mom with holy water.

"God,
Help Florence discover your peace.
Let her receive your comfort.
Help her be at rest knowing that you care for her,
and that you love her.
Calm her soul as she moves into the afterlife.
May she spend eternity with you.
May she live forever in your presence.
Amen."

And then we talk to her. We tell her how much we love her but that it's okay for her to let go. That she is safe and loved and not to be afraid and that my father and her sister are waiting for her. It is a time for saying anything left unsaid, and reiterating what she already knew – that we loved her and that she was safe.

Later in the evening, as we are getting dinner ready, I decide to go check on Mom. To me it looks like her chest is not rising and falling. The room is dark, so I turn on the light and again check her chest.

At this point Lynn enters the room.

"I can't tell if she's breathing," I say.

My sister leans down, listens, and places her hand on Mom's chest. "She is not breathing. She's gone."

We are prepared, but never prepared, to lose a loved one, especially someone who is such an important piece of who we are, indeed a piece of us. We cannot stop the tears from pouring out as we sigh and moan in grief, grateful that she is at peace, yet missing her already. This has been a heartbreaking, difficult, almost impossible time, yet we were called to pay it forward and ease her passing.

While we wait for the hospice nurse to arrive, we gather at Mom's bedside, stroke her hair, hold her hand, and kiss her forehead. Through the tears, we all tell her how much we love her. There are no words to express the loss that I feel at this moment; wanting to keep her here a little longer, and at the same time needing to let her go. It is a raw moment of reliving every moment of my life and thanking her silently for always being there and always loving me.

Epilogue

❖⸺❖

My sister and I attended to all the arrangements, meeting with the funeral home where my father's wake was held all those years ago. The pain of revisiting that time was only quieted by knowing that these two beautiful souls were now reunited.

We picked out a beautiful casket for mom, one decorated with scenes from the Last Supper. In gathering photographs for the wake, I was comforted by thoughts of what a full and beautiful life she had had.

Mom always said she wanted a closed casket. "I don't want anyone staring at me," she said. We initially picked out a dress for her to wear, one that she had worn to one of her granddaughter's weddings, but later decided that she should be in a comfy sweatsuit and her slippers, the way we wanted to remember her. When the funeral director escorted us into the room where Mom was laid out, we could not stop the tears from flowing. Through her tears, my sister said, "She doesn't look like herself," and she didn't. It was then we decided to have the casket closed as to remember her as she was, while also honoring her wishes. After putting a small bottle of vodka in the casket with her – a martini was her drink of choice – we asked the director to close the casket.

The wake was a testament to how many lives Mom touched. Relatives that we hadn't seen in years, friends of myself and Lynn and our children, work colleagues, all came out to remember her and stand by us in our grief. So many people came to pay their respects and support our family, and as a family we took much solace in comforting each other. Memories of my childhood come flooding back as if in an 8 millimeter film, one that my grandfather would take at every holiday. Memories frozen in time, thankful for the family that I'm a part of.

We had met with the priest who would attend to the wake and funeral beforehand so that he could know a little about Mom. With truth and beauty, his words captured so much of Mom's spirit and left us knowing that she would live on in our memories. Both Lynn and

I did a reading, as did my niece. I knew I had to do this for my mom and for all those gathered to celebrate and honor her, so I kept my tears at bay at best I could and stoically and precisely read God's words, speaking to all those gathered.

A reading from the Letter of Saint Paul to the Philippians:

> *"Rejoice in the Lord always.*
> *I shall say it again: rejoice!*
> *The Lord is near.*
>
> *Have no anxiety at all, but in everything, by prayer and petition, with thanksgiving, make your requests known to God.*
>
> *Then the peace of God that surpasses all understanding will guard your hearts and minds in Christ Jesus.*
>
> *Finally, whatever is true, whatever is honorable, whatever is just, or pure or lovely, whatever is gracious, if there is any excellence and if there is anything worthy of praise, think about these things. Keep on doing what you have learned and received and heard and seen in me. Then the God of peace will be with you."*

The word of the Lord. Thanks be to God.

Mom's been gone two weeks and every time I think of her, I shake my head in disbelief, as if this will make it all go away. I cannot believe she's gone—someone who has been such a part of your life for so long and suddenly they are not there. I think of calling her multiple times a day. When I'm cooking dinner, I think *Mom would like this*. When I am going up or down a flight of stairs, I think, *This is going to be hard for Mom*. Every plane that flies overhead reminds me of her. I think of her most often as she was when she was well, but the images of her last days and weeks that come creeping into my brain are hard to ignore.

***

Almost two months have now passed since Mom passed, and I miss her deeply. When things remind me of her, at first I embrace it, but then I do not allow myself to ponder as the loss causes too much pain and has left such a void.

I used to think that you could not fully be an "adult" until your parents were gone. And now I realize I was wrong. I am nothing if I'm not my mother's daughter. Yes, now maybe I can make some decisions without wondering what she would think, but even in her absence she is guiding me. Yet I feel untethered, with no one here for me to fall back on as the older, wiser one. Burdens all fall on my shoulders now. A strange feeling of being a grown woman, but still a child.

Eight months since Mom's passing and the pain felt by her loss has not diminished. I still think I should call her, and I miss the times we spent together. She has sent me signs, though, and I continue to feel her presence.

In all the memories and things she left behind, I am reminded of how lucky I was to call her Mom. And I take comfort in knowing that during her last days she was surrounded by the family that loved her and that she felt safe and cared for. Surprising that a time filled with so much worry and sadness could be such a blessing and a gift.

So, what have I learned in the past six months?

Life truly is a circle.

I'm stronger than I thought.

It really does take a village.

Don't "wait until tomorrow" to spend time with family, call a friend, tell someone you love them.

And one more thing... I wish this book was longer.

www.ingramcontent.com/pod-product-compliance
Lightning Source LLC
Chambersburg PA
CBHW030045100526
44590CB00011B/336